Our Holidays

Celebrate Independence Day

Amy Hayes

Cavendish Square

New York

Published in 2015 by Cavendish Square Publishing, LLC
243 5th Avenue, Suite 136, New York, NY 10016

Website: cavendishsq.com

This publication represents the opinions and views of the author based on his or her personal experience, knowledge, and research. The information in this book serves as a general guide only. The author and publisher have used their best efforts in preparing this book and disclaim liability rising directly or indirectly from the use and application of this book.

CPSIA Compliance Information: Batch #WW15CSQ

All websites were available and accurate when this book was sent to press.

Library of Congress Cataloging-in-Publication Data

Hayes, Amy.
Celebrate Independence Day / Amy Hayes.
pages cm. — (Our holidays)
Includes index.
ISBN 978-1-50260-234-3 (hardcover) ISBN 978-1-50260-232-9 (paperback) ISBN 978-1-50260-228-2 (ebook)
1. Fourth of July—Juvenile literature. I. Title.

E286.A1352 2015
394.2634—dc23

2014032630

Senior Copy Editor: Wendy A. Reynolds
Art Director: Jeffrey Talbot
Designer: Joseph Macri
Senior Production Manager: Jennifer Ryder-Talbot
Production Editor: David McNamara
Photo Researcher: J8 Media

The photographs in this book are used by permission and through the courtesy of:
Cover photo by Tetra Images/Getty Images; WorldPictures/Shutterstock.com, 5; Culture Club/Hulton Archive/Getty Images, 7; Maria Bell/Shutterstock.com, 9; ©iStockphoto.com/bill oxford, 11; Stockbyte/Thinkstock, 13; Thinkstock Images/Stockbyte/Getty Images, 15; ©iStockphoto.com/Kali9, 17; Dmytro Shevchenko/iStock/Thinkstock, 19; gary718/Shutterstock.com, 21.

Printed in the United States of America

Contents

Today is **Independence** Day!

4

5

Independence Day is the birthday of our country.

We celebrate the United States on Independence Day.

Independence Day happens every year on July 4th.

Today is July 4th.

JULY

Sunday	Monday	Tuesday	Wednesday	Thursday	Friday	Saturday
				1	2	3
4	5	6	7	8	9	10
11	12	13	14	15	16	17
18	19	20	21	22	23	24
25	26	27	28	29	30	31

9

We are going to celebrate.

We will have a flag **ceremony**.

We will need a flag.

11

We raise the flag.

It is way up high.

13

We say the
Pledge of Allegiance.

Now it is time to celebrate!

On Independence Day,
we have a **barbecue**.

17

Then we go and see
the **fireworks**.

The fireworks go "bang!"

They are very pretty.

19

Happy Independence Day!

20

New Words

barbecue (BAR-be-kew) Cooking and eating outside.

ceremony (SAIR-e-mo-nee) A special or important event.

fireworks (FYER-werkz) Things that explode to make light and noise at a celebration.

independence (in-dee-PEN-dens) Being free from the control of others.

Pledge of Allegiance (PLEJ OF a-LEE-jens) Words that are said to show support for the country.

Index

About the Author

Amy Hayes lives in the beautiful city of Buffalo. She usually celebrates Independence Day on the beach with her family.

About

Bookworms help independent readers gain reading confidence through high-frequency words, simple sentences, and strong picture/text support. Each book explores a concept that helps children relate what they read to the world they live in.